North Pole South Pole

Nancy Smiler Levinson

illustrated by
Diane Dawson Hearn

Weddell seal and young

SCHOLASTIC INC.

New York Toronto London Auckland Sydney
Mexico City New Delhi Hong Kong Buenos Aires

For Regina Griffin
N. S. L.

For my daughters, Leana and Melanie
D. D. H.

On the cover:
(top) polar bear;
(bottom) Emperor penguins

ISBN 0-439-58745-X

12 11 10 9 8 7 6 5 4 3 2   3 4 5 6 7 8/0
Printed in the U.S.A.   23

First Scholastic printing, November 2003

thick-billed
murres

This is our world—
the planet Earth.

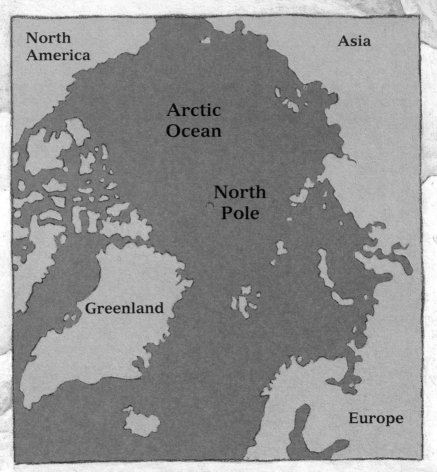

North America

Asia

Arctic Ocean

North Pole

Greenland

Europe

The Arctic

The top of the earth is called
the Arctic.
The North Pole is at the Arctic center.
This pole is the farthest point north.

The bottom of the earth
is called Antarctica.
The South Pole
is in the Antarctic.
This pole is the farthest point south.

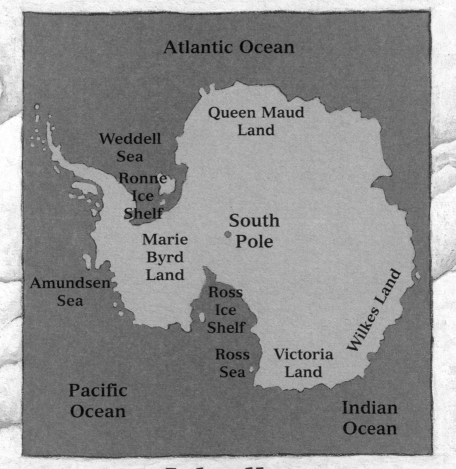

Antarctica

An imaginary line runs
between the poles.
It is called an axis.
The earth spins on its axis.
This gives us day and night.
The earth also revolves around the sun.
As the earth spins and revolves,
we get changing seasons of the year.

killer whale

The Arctic and Antarctic
are polar regions.
The sun rays do not shine directly
on the poles.
The poles are the coldest places
on Earth.

It is too cold for rain at the poles.
Snow falls. It falls year after year.
The snow turns into great masses
of ice that are always moving.

snow buntings

The air at the poles is dry.

The frozen land is empty.

Both places are cold deserts.

What do you see at the poles?

Ice. Snow. White space.

You can see your breath

turn to icy crystals in midair.

If there is a blizzard,

you can't see anything at all.

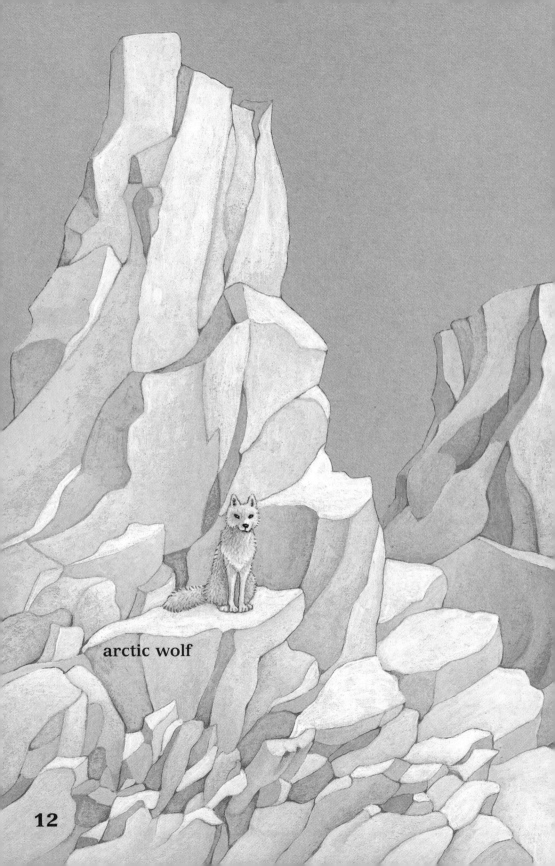

arctic wolf

NORTH POLE

The North Pole is water
surrounded by land.
The water is the Arctic Ocean.
It is always covered by ice.
Winter temperatures drop to
50 degrees *below* zero.
Your glasses's metal frames
could freeze to your face!

beluga whale

The Arctic region has summer, too.
Warm streams of water
move up from the Atlantic Ocean.
They bring milder weather.

walrus

In summer the temperatures rise to
40 degrees *above* zero.
That is warm enough
to thaw a frozen fish.

harp seal

The earth tilts as it revolves
around the sun.
In winter the North Pole
tilts *away* from the sun.
The Arctic gets no daylight then.
From October to March
it is dark all the time.
In summer the North Pole
tilts *toward* the sun.
The sun never sets.
From April to September
it is light all the time.
You could go fishing
at midnight.

Arctic
summer

Arctic
winter

snowshoe hare

polar bear

arctic fox

Who is the king of animals
in the Arctic?
The mighty polar bear!
Whales, seals, and walrus
swim in the Arctic waters, too.

gray whale

walrus

harp seals

Land surrounds the Arctic Ocean.
The deep soil of the land
stays frozen all year.
No trees grow.
But mosses, flowers, and berries
grow every summer.

arctic wolf

arctic poppies

king eider duck

Caribou, arctic foxes, and wolves
make their home on Arctic land.
Ducks and seabirds come in summer.
They feed on fish, plants, and insects
near ocean shores.

white-rumped sandpiper

caribou

rock ptarmigan

arctic daisies

People have lived in the Far North
for thousands of years.
They hunt and fish for their food.
They made their clothing
and tents from animal skins.

Scientists and explorers come
to the North Pole, too.
They need layers of warm clothing.
They also need loads of food.
They eat chocolate
and peanut butter for energy.

The air is so dry,
they get very thirsty.
They need to melt enough ice
to drink three quarts of water a day.

black-browed albatross

SOUTH POLE

The South Pole is on land
surrounded by water.
This land is the continent
of Antarctica.
Most of it is covered with ice
that is two miles thick.
Even mountains, volcanoes, and lakes
are covered with ice.
Ice at the South Pole never melts.

chinstrap penguins

Dry air crackles. Winds howl.
Temperatures fall to 128 degrees
below zero!
Water freezes instantly.
Toothpaste and flashlight batteries
freeze.

Adélie penguins

Metal tools snap in half.
It is so cold that food never rots.
Antarctica is the coldest
place of all.

Antarctic seasons are the opposite
of seasons in the north.
June and July are the middle of winter.
It is dark all the time.
December and January
are the middle of summer.
There is daylight all the time.
Summer temperatures
at the South Pole
stay *below* zero.

Antarctic winter   Antarctic summer

cormorant

31

No land animals live at the South Pole.
Only the Weddell seal and an insect
called the midge live in Antarctica
all year.
Penguins and other seabirds
come there in the summer months.
Penguins ride on moving ice floes.
Layers of fat keep them warm.
Tightly packed feathers keep them dry.

Weddell seals

Emperor penguins

No people are native to Antarctica.
They could not have survived.
Now scientists from all over the world
come and live in research stations.
They need generators
to create power and heat.

They need all their food
delivered by air or sea.
They also need snowmobiles
to get from place to place.
On most winter days
they cannot go outside at all.

The North and South Poles
are places for scientists
to study the earth.
Scientists study the ice.
They study how weather changes
and how wildlife survives.
They study the earth's past
and think about its future.

They are looking for ways
to protect our earth
for all living things.

NORTH POLE

—It is in the Arctic.

—It is water surrounded by land.

—The average temperature
in winter is 22 to 32 degrees below zero.

—The average temperature inland in summer
is 32 to 50 degrees above zero.

—Winter months are October to March.

—Summer months are April to September.

—The first recorded explorer to reach the
North Pole by dogsled was Admiral Robert
E. Peary in 1909.

—The first pilot to fly over the North Pole
was Admiral Richard E. Byrd in 1926.

SOUTH POLE

—It is in the Antarctic.

—It is on land surrounded by water.

—Antarctica is a continent.

—The average temperature of the interior in winter is 76 degrees below zero.

—The average temperature of the interior in summer is 14 degrees below zero.

—Winter months are April to September.

—Summer months are October to March.

—The first explorer to reach the South Pole by dogsled was Roald Amundsen in 1911.

—The first pilot to fly over the South Pole was Admiral Richard E. Byrd in 1929.

Acknowledgments

For their expert assistance and goodwill

in the preparation of this book, the author thanks

Linda Duguay, Director of Environmental Studies,

University of Southern California;

David Friscic, Technical Information Specialist,

Office of Polar Programs, National Science Foundation;

and Donal T. Manahan, Dean of Research,

College of Letters, Arts, and Sciences,

University of Southern California, and Chair,

Polar Research Board of National Academies.

baby harp seal